MW01000463

How Are You Feeling Today?

By Chip Dodd, PhD

Illustrations by Shelley Dieterichs

Scripture quotations are from the ESV® Bible
(The Holy Bible, English Standard Version®),
copyright © 2001 by Crossway, a publishing
ministry of Good News Publishers.
Used by permission. All rights reserved.

Printed in the United States.

ISBN: 979-8-9854515-0-4

**Chip Dodd
Resources**

chipdodd.com

Check out the QR
Code in the back of the
book for a video gift

Introduction

I was invited by Christian educators to synthesize my book, *The Voice of the Heart*, into the simplest form possible for young children. *How Are You Feeling Today?* is the result.

You and I are designed as emotional and spiritual creatures who are created to live fully, even in a broken, tragic world. We live fully by being in relationship with ourselves, our heads and hearts connected, in relationship with others, and especially, in relationship with God. We have been given feelings as tools to use that can move us to remain connected to ourselves, others, and God. The Psalms are a great example of this truth.

How Are You Feeling Today? is a small children's book that is part of a large mission—to help children embrace core values and express behaviors consistent with those values in an ever-changing, challenging world. We want children to know, grow in, and trust the truth of the seminal verse, "Above all else, guard your heart, for everything you do flows from it" (Prov. 4:23). As children's minds are being educated, so will they also learn the social and emotional skills that allow them fully to share their gifts in a world that needs them.

My prayer is that children will remain connected to how God created them and continue to be known by those they love and who love them—especially the God who knitted them together with unending love.

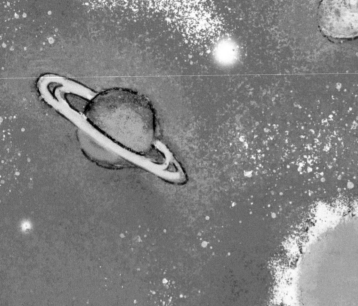

In the beginning,
God created the
heavens and the earth.

Genesis 1:1

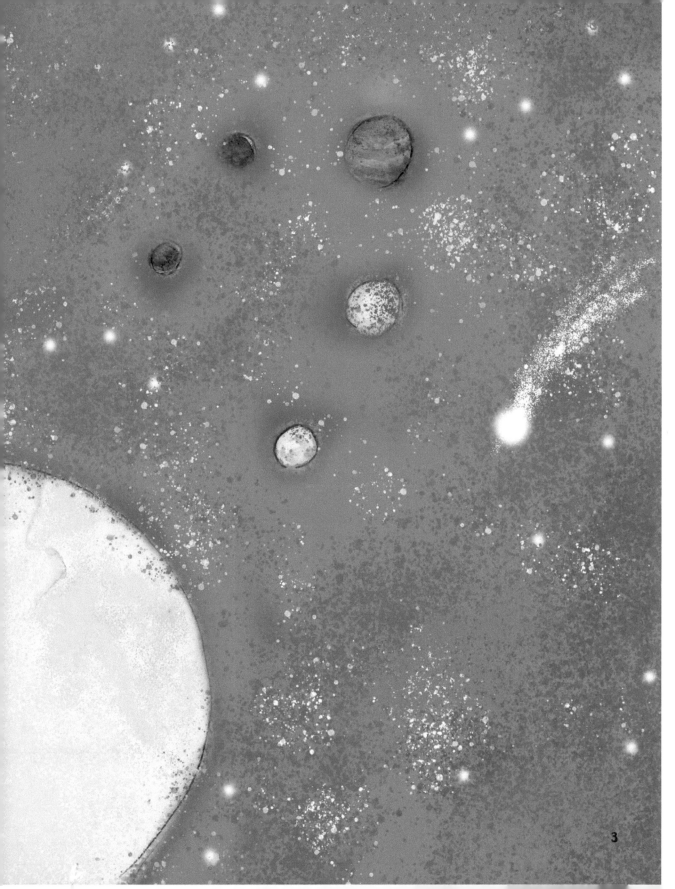

God also
created
you and me.

I praise you, for I am fearfully
and wonderfully made.
Wonderful are
your works; my soul
knows it very well.

Psalm 139:14

4

God sent His Son, Jesus,
to come be with us
because when you love someone,
you want to be with them
and care for them.

For God so loved the world,
that he gave his only Son,
that whoever believes in him
should not perish
but have eternal life.

John 3:16

When we read the
Bible and when we learn
more about Jesus, we
understand God wants us
to love Him, to love others,
and to love ourselves.

God wants us to love
with our whole hearts.

God gave us our heart and
filled it with feelings.

God gave us hearts and feelings
to help us live well.

We live in a world where wonderful things happen.
We live in a world where painful things happen.

God made us able to laugh and to cry.
God made us able to be calm and to be scared.

God made us this way so
we could share the feelings
of our hearts with God and
others who care.

How do you know exactly what you are feeling?

Sometimes, it can be confusing.
Sometimes, you have more than one feeling at the same time!

It is good to tell God and people who love you
the feelings in your heart.

God gave us feelings to help us.

Have you ever felt any of these?

FEAR

LONELY

ANGER

GUILT

SHAME

Let's learn more about each feeling.

GLAD

When we feel glad, we are joyful, hopeful, and secure.
We feel gladness when something we have waited for,
longed for, and worked for happens!

Sometimes you feel glad when

you score a goal

you find a special shell at the beach

you share a toy with a friend

you make a new friend

you remember a time with your family

When we are glad, we sometimes
smile, laugh, dance, cheer, worship, praise, share, hug

When you feel glad, what can you do?
Share what you learn.
Smile at other people.
Do something kind — like picking a flower for a friend.
Color a picture for someone who
isn't feeling very glad.

And always,
tell God about your
gladness,
and thank Him
for being with you.

SAD

Sometimes we feel sad. We can feel sad when something happens we did not want to happen. Sadness tells us we need comfort from people who love us and from God.

Sometimes you feel sad when

a friend moves to another place

a pet dies

the game is canceled because of rain

you move away from your old school

you try to build something, and it breaks

When we feel sad, we sometimes
cry
choose to be by ourselves
don't want to talk
decide to quit
cover our faces
hesitate to try new things

When you feel sad, what can you do?
Tell a parent or someone who loves you and ask for help.
Write a story about what happened and how you feel.
Pray for other people who may be feeling sad.

And always,
tell God about your
sadness,
and thank Him for
being with you.

HURT

Sometimes we feel hurt. Hurt lets us know that we have pain.
The hurt can be physical — like a scraped knee.
Hurt can also be a feeling in our hearts.

Sometimes you feel hurt when

someone says something unkind to you
someone makes fun of you and everyone else laughs
you aren't chosen for the team
a friend doesn't want to be with you

When we feel hurt, we sometimes

cry
want to be by ourselves
pretend we don't hurt
say mean things to others
stop doing things we used to like doing

When you feel hurt, what can you do?

Tell someone who loves you how you feel.

Say, "Please stop" or tell a teacher or parent
if someone is being mean to you or others.

Draw a picture of what happened.

Ask someone who loves you to talk about a time
he or she felt hurt and talk together about what to do.

Spend time with a kind friend.

And always,
tell God about your hurt,
and thank Him for being with you.

FEAR

Sometimes we feel fear.
Fear tells us something we don't
want to happen might happen.

Sometimes you feel fear when

you are in the dark
there is a big storm
you see a dog that growls and looks mean
you have to take a test
your parents are upset or arguing
you ride a roller coaster

When we feel fear, we sometimes
hide, become quiet, cry, worry, feel ill, hesitate

When you feel fear, what can you do?
Ask for help.
Think about times when everything turned out all right.
Talk about it with someone who loves you.
Learn more about what makes you afraid
and what you can do about it.

And always,
tell God about your fear,
and thank Him for being with you.

LONELY

Sometimes we feel lonely.
Loneliness tells us we need God and other people.
We can feel lonely when we don't share
the feelings of our hearts with
people we love or with God.

Sometimes you feel lonely when

your parents are away on a trip
your friends are too busy to be with you
you don't know how to do something that others enjoy
you don't think anyone understands how you feel

When we feel lonely, we sometimes

choose to be alone

try hard to get attention

don't care about something that used to be important

feel bored

When you feel lonely, what can you do?

Talk about it with someone who loves you.

Pray.

Write down how you feel.

Spend time with a friend.

Do something kind for someone else who might feel lonely.

And always,

tell God about your loneliness,

and thank Him for being with you.

23

ANGER

Sometimes we feel anger. Anger is a feeling that tells us
we care about something a lot, or we really want something to be different.
Anger is energy that can be used in the right way to make things
better even though it might be hard.

Sometimes you feel angry when

a difficult project fails

you lose the race

you see someone treated unfairly

you study hard because you really want to learn

When we feel angry, we sometimes

use words we regret

stay brave

invite someone who is being left out to join in the group

refuse to participate

try to fix the problem

think about what could have happened

When you feel angry, what can you do?

Use the energy to keep trying.

Take time to learn about the reason you are angry.

Find a quiet place to think until you feel more calm.

Talk with someone you love about how you are feeling.

Decide if there's something you can do
to make the situation better now or next time.

Ask for help so you can accomplish what you want to do.

And always,

tell God about your anger,
and thank Him for being with you.

GUILT

Sometimes we feel guilt. Guilt is a feeling that tells us
we did something wrong. Guilt helps us ask
for forgiveness and say, "I'm sorry."

Sometimes you feel guilt when

you say mean things that hurt others

you choose to tell a lie

you know something is wrong, and you do it anyway

you don't listen to God

When we feel guilt, we sometimes

hide from others

blame others or make excuses

feel sad

avoid looking in the eyes of another person
who might know what we did

When you feel guilt,
what can you do?

Ask for forgiveness.
Tell the truth.
Say, "I'm sorry."
Ask for help.

And always,

tell God about your guilt,
and thank Him
for being with you.

SHAME

Sometimes we feel shame. Healthy shame is a feeling
that lets us know we can't live life alone — and that's okay.

Sometimes you feel shame when

you make a mistake

you need help

you don't know all the answers

you ask questions

When we feel shame, we sometimes

don't want to talk with others

ask for help

keep our mistakes a secret

When you feel shame, what can you do?

You can tell someone you love how you feel.

You can admit your mistakes or weaknesses.

You can try again.

You can read stories about other people
and what they learned from their mistakes or weaknesses.

Accept how God made you.

And always,
tell God about your shame,
and thank Him for
being with you.

We live in a world where wonderful things happen.

We live in a world where painful things happen.

Remember:

Feel your feelings

Tell the truth

And give it to God

Humble yourselves, therefore, under the mighty hand of God
so that at the proper time he may exalt you, casting all your
anxieties on him, because he cares for you.

1 Peter 5:6-7

Do not be anxious about anything, but in everything
by prayer and supplication with thanksgiving
let your requests be made known to God.
And the peace of God, which surpasses all
understanding, will guard your hearts
and your minds in Christ Jesus.

Philippians 4:6-7

To the Grownups,

All of us are created as people who feel and think. We are
also created to find fulfillment in relationships with others
and God. All of us, older people and children, feel. When
we lose connection to our feelings, we become impaired.
We remove ourselves from gifts we were created to have in
truthful and genuine relationships. By facing, naming, and
sharing our feelings, we can experience the fullness of living
as God created us. To learn more about feelings, please read,
The Voice of the Heart – A Call to Full Living. It is the
grownup version of *How Are You Feeling Today?*

Your children will be glad that you joined them.

Sincerely,

Chip

The EIGHT FEELINGS

IMPAIRMENT Less True (Not Wrong)	TRUTH	Gifts of TRUTH Gifts of Feelings
I am not happy.	GLAD	I like me, others, and God.
No one cares about me.	SAD	I care a lot. I am cared about.
I want to get even.	HURT	I feel better and braver.
I feel nervous. I am anxious.	FEAR	I trust others' help, and I trust God.
I feel unloved. I feel alone.	LONELY	I am a friend. I have a friend.
I don't care. I don't matter.	ANGER	I keep on caring and hoping.
I am unacceptable.	GUILT	I say, "I'm sorry."
I don't matter. I am unlovable.	SHAME	I make mistakes. I ask for help.

We Develop the Gifts of Truth by:

Naming what we feel.

Telling God and someone who cares about us what we feel.

Believing that God and others will be with us and help us.

Thank you so much for purchasing ***How Are You Feeling Today***!
As a special gift to you, please use the QR code below to watch a free,
45-minute talk from Dr. Chip Dodd on how you can explore
The Eight Feelings further with your child.